T0194190

POEMS, PASSAGES
&
REAL HEARTFELT SHIT

by George

authorHOUSE®

AuthorHouse™
1663 Liberty Drive
Bloomington, IN 47403
www.authorhouse.com
Phone: 1 (800) 839-8640

Published by AuthorHouse 02/04/2020

ISBN: 978-1-7283-4649-6 (sc)
ISBN: 978-1-7283-4648-9 (e)

Contents

Introduction

It's true- these aren't your normal, everyday, average poems, passages, and verses. Allow me to share. I used to believe words meant absolutely *nothing*- that actions spoke much louder than mere stuttered sounds coming from one's rambling piss hole of a mouth. And that can certainly be true. Especially with shitheads who just talk a good game, but can never back it up, deliver on their promises, or just stand by what they preach.

(*Do motherfucker. Don't just stand there and talk. Such as* politicians, dead beat dads, liars, big mouth tough guys, drunk fucks and every other shit talking, inconsiderate, unapologetic, no blinker using- lane changing, *I drive a better car than you so I don't have to watch out for your safety,* selfish, worthless fuck, we run into every day.) Feel me? Don't talk motherfucker... DO.

However, as I grew into my gray hair days, I began to notice how words can touch and have more worth than I actually thought. (Such as verbalizing *'fuck you'* instead of using your finger. It just has way more impact, plus you feel better.) I think it's because I had a rough childhood and words were pointless and didn't matter. If my father was going to break his foot off in my ass, a well worded plea or compliment about the deeper part of his character or his incredibly hard receding hair line wasn't going to stop him from doing so. Just saying. I had always found words to be useless, always fake, said to please people in the moment.

But I've changed my thinking, *as we all should from time to time,* and I evolved. I now believe in taking the opportunity to express what's important to oneself. Words can be a wonderfully artistic creation.

Lastly, I want to add, there's no genius in these writings. There's no claim to fame, just a fun hobby of mine and instead of letting them sit around in a hard drive, I thought I'd share them. Maybe you'll find them entertaining. Maybe even inspiring. Maybe that's fucking reaching.

<u>Stardust</u>

Electric stars shape distant galaxies. Beacons by design,
they exist as oases of light planted deep in the deserts of
dark space and time. Eventually they explode becoming
forgotten memories, falling as magical embers, making
up the grand scenery, shaping into entities. Creating
all we know, maybe that's why they call to me.
I feel my feet dug firmly into earth, magnetized,
weighed down since birth, but my hand reaches into
the atmosphere, leading the way through layers of
broken air as I rocket past Venus, then faster I fly past
Jupiter's moons and head straight for Andromeda's core.
I want more, I want to explore the planets unknown-
to write exciting letters telling everyone back home,
I did it. I reached for the stars and I survived.
How great would that be... to accomplish ones dreams
before fading into memories.

Behold

It's been said throughout time and believed by greater
minds, that we don't just walk an endless mile. It's
not some unknown path or a hap-hazzardous trek.
It's been deemed the ultimate test. A judged journey, a
different kind of quest, with its focus more on chances
than it is on distance. So much so, that the distance
is just a mere gift. For instance; the 'chances' I speak
of are to prove who you are in character make up; the
negligence you can't hide, deny or fake. No matter how
rich or massive your ego or intellect, broken down to
the simplest of concepts, it is of the utmost importance,
your highest concern be that of others before yourself,
even the strangers that surround you in abundance.

It's said to be written in stone, although no one
truly knows who we are or where we come from;
these words still resonate and are to be passed
down for each soul to understand and know.
So behold, and let it be told;
The riches you seek are frivolous. Material items
are worthless. You're time is recorded and your
journey is weighed in selfless progress.

So keep laughing at others, keep ignoring your brothers,
keep thinking you're better. Keep acting like there's no
consequences that will be kept and paid to the letter.
Keep buying useless goods. Keep doing all the stupid shit
you do instead of what you should. There's a balance in
life, of course. However, instead of running your mouth,
pretending you're special, look in the mirror first, and
think about the chances you've squandered and missed.
We will all be judged, punished and shamed, and right
now, you know in your heart exactly who to blame.

<u>Floor Plan</u>

I've had this conversation before,
deep down in my core. I'm worth a lot more than what
they've cashed me in for. I work at it everyday, avoid
being a burden in anyway. I'm better, smarter, I try so
hard to fly so high, sometimes on fire, and not in a good
way. I've traveled through time farther than my father,
to savor the flavor of life and all it has to offer.
I continue to fight harder in my mind to reach the levels I
know I can find and achieve with belief and finally receive
what's coming to me, and not necessarily financially. So
many have taken from me, disrespectfully knocked me
down and kicked around what was left of me. X-rated
my life without asking, raped the smile right off of me,
berated my tries and labeled my existence a catastrophe.
Betrayed and belittled, back-stabbed and in the middle
of it all, equated me to nothing, said I was a symphony
of self destruction. Looked down at me as if I were crust,
mere dust that had grown from old mold and blown-in
from winds off rusted tin cans in a garbage bin. I've busted
in and kicked the door down. Open your eyes, recognize
this new floor plan laid out in plain site, this souls in mid
flight, I'm done talking about what I might. It's time to
make this last stand and take what's rightfully mine.

Wondrous

Beyond majestic in splendid creation. Intricately detailed from harmonious inception. Each hemisphere brilliantly astounds while beauty gleams through magnificent inspiration. Woven into complexity, a tapestry of love and light are the strengths and might behind the guiding voices that carry us through the depths of cold and the treachery of darkness injected into our lives. World's apart from any other, there's no denying her victorious standalone. She's an incredible heavenly wonder, every one of us, call home.

Expected to maintain a propensity, she's hardwired in a proclivity to carry on her master design to survive for all eternity. To create goals, formulate conclusions and paths to lead and conquer. We drink from the abundant rivers of illusion and ecstasy as they ebb and flow through mountainous imagination. We climb in recreation, in search of answers, and test her very limits and boundaries; it's our only true destiny.

However under carnivorous examine she endures constant scrutiny. If abandoned, she'll wander aimlessly, helpless to progress, often misdiagnosed, trapped within the confines of her own fortress, sometimes forever lost in ridicule and madness. She can be in control of everything, or simply nothing, but she'll constantly graze on new ideas for growth to keep us from the wicked grip of sadness. She thrives and lives within us all, as the drive behind our lives, she's the amazing, magical, wondrous mind.

Battlefield

Souls lose their way, even their lives in cut throat fights. Wide eyes watch and fall to pieces as their innocence is caught in the cross fire. Tears fall, cries turn into shrieks of terror as hatred explodes. All the while, tensions grow in the cold dark shadows. Assets become bargaining chips, disputes exist that no one can possibly win, yet they carry on with missiles of regret no matter the collateral damage to kin. Another skirmish ensues, who's wrong and who's right. Rage takes center stage, multiple shots fired long into the battle torn nights... life and love expire. Orders issued. Love stories turn into sad stories. Hands that once held each other with plans of 'victory and peace' so high you could feel the joy inside of a well thought out future, so tangible within reach and sight, now lose their grip, giving up, letting go of all that mattered as supplies get cut off from the front lines. The wounded limp off the battlefield holding what's left of their hearts as they bleed. They've given life and limb, blood sweat and tears. Thrown into territory uncharted. Divorce was never imagined before the battle started.

Hanging by a Thread

I am barely standing from the wars we wage.
I don't even know why I fight or what I'm
fighting for anymore these days.
It's a desperate nightmare we've engaged in.
The battles never over,
it's always in disguise as peace time,
lurking behind, fake smiles,
and miles and miles of denial
make up the road of frustration,
in need of a course correction.
Maybe, no I'm sure
I'm fighting for more than just my life,
we're running out of time.
it's do or die.
I won't deny that I'm no angel, I won't even
say I've never caused you any pain.
The more I obsess and think about it, the more I put
my self in danger and dig my own emotional grave.
There are those who mentally wander deserts forever,
searching for the light that shines the way
to a path that's better,
where the fabric of life isn't torn and frayed.
I've climbed mountains and I have seen the rains.
I've weathered storms that could carry you away,
but here you are, wake up and see this life
for what it is and what it's for.
No more relying on time to heal wounds.
Let's stop living in a dream world to feel good.
If you don't want this anymore, then it's dead
and that's okay, but say the word, don't keep me
hanging by a thread, cuz if I had the choice
I'd choose 'us' over me, instead.

Shelf-life

It felt like the right thing to do at the time. Looking back, I ask how then, could it turn out to be the worst decision of my life? I was over the moon. I put everything I had into the forever we chose. I gave all I could. I sacrificed and became another so others could. I gave til it hurt, because that's what you do. You buy, lavish, pay and work, ignore you're own needs so the garden can flourish. But nights are spent alone. Fights claw to the bone. Behind doors you silently cry, while anger grows, slowly turning you from resilient to stone. You're left with nothing but an awful taste in your mouth and you suddenly realize there's a 'shelf life' to this thing you once praised out loud. You pray for a miracle to lift the cloud of frustration, depression and anger that is forever looming, constantly growing, feeding the darkness that's consuming. You beg for the dark days to end. But sadly, they go on for years, they go on without mend. The pain inside is muffled by 'time and tears' as the days turn into the "Never agains". This one burned so bad I can hardly breathe without sighing. I'm so tired of working. I'm worn out from fighting. I can't take any more lying. Inside I can actually feel myself dying. I don't even recognize who I am in the mirror. All I know is I'm done with this endeavor. There's nothing left of me, nothing left to give. I don't even want to live. I have never been so betrayed and spit on. I'm scratching to survive, crawling to find energy and light. I'm barely alive. I've lost count of the tears I've cried. One day I'll try to find the strength to smile, for now, I'll just wonder how love could turn so sour.

Life-blood

In depth, I see myself competing with the moon.
In breadth, I span like a musical tune, spreading lazily
yet hastily moving toward my goal. Freely roaming,
foaming at the mouth. I can kick harder than a mule.
I'm deeper than most give me credit for. I'm constantly
running, trying to reach new ground, achieve new
heights, without fright, for not even fear could stop me.
I am the crave that pumps the life blood into the soul.
I am the sexy temptress, the goddess of will, the burning
instilled, wearing high heels in the cold. I am young,
I am old, faster I climb, spreading my crest. I live
naked in your breath. I'm infatuation at it's best. I'm
smarter and craftier than you think. I've ruled the world
since time could drink in the seconds. My body is the
reflection of your inner workings. My name slides right
off your tongue, they call me the drive that is the fire,

I am the she that is *Desire*.

Log Cabin

As cold winds roared outside, a hearty fire crackled
on indoors, insisting we rest for the night. We'd all
sit in colorful flannel and pour out our stories til
restlessness settled. Becoming hypnotized by the fire's
soothing dance on red hot logs, we'd watch flames
fight for height. Relaxed, were our weary bodies in
it's promising warmth, as it told us the day was over
and we could forget the chores we had so diligently
accomplished in depth. We had the right to rest.
At least til morning- is what the night had
said with it's cold, darkened, tired breath,
whispering against the back of my head.
The great room held our loving huddle as we waited for
the heat to sink into our bones. Before we'd all go to bed
to dream, we'd burn a pile of logs and make sure we all
had enough to eat. We wore blankets like gowns and
had plenty of slippers and soft pajamas to go around.
It reminded me of when I was young and had a lot to
learn. It was the only time we gathered. The rest of the
year we couldn't be bothered. Thankfully, the winters
continue to bring us together as we cuddle in silence
annually, breathing in the solidarity of family our
father instilled in us before he left. He hated the fast
paced city and was the reason he built this wonderful
gift for us, on a cold Vermont mountaintop, instead.

An Invitation

There's a reason we fight for what's sustainable
or reach for what's unobtainable.
There's a reason we hold onto what's sentimental
and don't dismiss what's unfavorable.
There's a reason we strive for excellence when
we're surrounded by the inevitable.
There's a reason we laugh at lightning
and scream back at thunder.
Yes, we're thick headed in sum, but there's a consistency in
our blood, mainly because we're the leaders our mothers
told us to be. We're the defenders of what we were bred
to believe, the protectors of our children and families.
A gift from mother nature to bring us to victory holding
all that we deem sacred, to make our mark in history.
That's why we get up everyday and persevere through
storms and press on through pain and misery.
We recognize that deliverance only lies in the hands
of those who reach out and make it happen.
Build, create, lead and sustain is the plan.
The future is in your hands. This is your chance.
Welcome to the world of Man.
You're cordially invited to do something grand.

Daughter

With countless tears wept, she learned at an early age how abandonment felt. Her father, a foolish man, walked out of her life, missing out on all that could be had, between a daughter and her dad. It's truly sad and the reason I came to her side. I didn't like the guy, but I held her tight, swallowed my pride and raised her like she was mine. 14 years later, she's older, wiser and beautiful as ever. She's got a good head on her shoulders and understands what I've done to save her. Even her mother left us and taught her a valuable lesson; blood isn't every thing. She's surprised I still care for her.

Now, I don't have all the answers, but I still hug and give her advice. Life's tough on its own, it's even tougher without a dad's voice to reassure and guide through dark nights, to be the rock that will stand the test of time. So I told her, you may not be of my blood, but I'll always be your father. We have history and laughter, and memories of Christmas's together. We have been a team forever. I don't care what anyone says, I'll always be your dad and you'll always be my daughter.

Blossom

Dick biscuit, fuck-stick and cunt-lick cannot be used to describe your grandmother. Limp-dick, skin-flap and sac-dragger are not to be used to address your grandfather. But we all know about your whore of a mother, who brought joy to so many others from shore to shore, making sure she sucked every dick so pure as if they all had the cure. She wanted nothing more than to be good in bed, and with a nickname like Red, how could she not be. She was always cock-heavy, a half lesbian lefty, a seasoned veteran, who let them all in. With a club foot and a pending hysterectomy, she used to beg me with that banged up pussy, that hung three inches below where it should be, to come over and stuff her like a thanksgiving turkey.

I declined all except one time...

and that's why you call me Daddy.

Space Ace & Monkey

Come in Space Ace, come in. This is ground control, the
only post that has your last communication. We also
know you're a dumb ass fool for taking this mission
instead of vacation. So listen. This station, hasn't heard
from you. It's day thirty-two. These men still have jobs
to do. Contact us soon or we're assuming you're losing
speed and you're off course; gone forever, wait, it gets
worse. You're lost together, left the ship and severed
your tether and whether you've followed your notes to
the letter all for the better, you're taking measures to
adjust. There 's emergency levers if you must, so get it
together and remember, it's Jupiter's moons or bust.

Now, this office is a hot box full of soft cocks wearing
black socks, eatin' tuna outta zip-locks, with bad
breath readin' desktops, sweatin like chicks wearing
crop tops in the back drop. But they're not. This is
serious and I mean this, you're approaching Venus
with only one engine working and it's freezin',
so believe me- you need us.

"This is Space Ace. I hear you loud and clear. You won't
believe what happened here. My circuits got fried when
Monkey pulled out his jungle dick and pissed inside
the capsule, ruining the module. He's a real asshole.
He ate all the food, took a shit and flung his poo into
my eye. I cried tears of shit and now I'm flying blind.
Who's idea was it to put a monkey in the sky by my
side. I can hear him jacking off and smiling as I vomit
in my helmet from the stench of hot monkey shit. I'll
be home real soon but first I'm dropping off that hairy
prick and his lumps of floating poo, on the moon."

You Ain't Shit

It's shocking that you're still doubting me, like I'm some
kind of moron spitting idiocy. Honestly, you need a
lobotomy. Shit's pent up inside of me, just waiting to get
outta me, and it's flowing like Shakespeare's diary, but for
some reason it's not good enough for your high society,
high and mighty intellect. But if I recollect, and don't
neglect to correct if I misdirect as I reflect, but the bed
you made has never left us amazed. You're words are tired,
you're a boring haze, fading fast, a pathetic blast from
the past. You're arthritic, you're passe at best and while
we're on the subject, you look like shit. That's not a cheap
shot, it's truth to the crock pot of crap that don't stop.
Please, lock up your mouth,
you're not, stocked in clout,
you're rock-bottoming out,
you're being, phased the fuck out,
you act like you're, from down south;
three biscuits and a bucket of chicken,
you couldn't suck a dick with someone elses mouth.

So next time please, don't talk shit in an others
direction, that's just a limp wristed, feeble attempt
with a limp dick erection to get attention.

How to become a Legend

Permeate the mind with positive action.
(Change your life with something interesting)
Permeate mankind with selfless dedication.
(Do something for someone else besides yourself.)
Caress the soul with emotional consideration.
(Show compassion you heartless shitfuck.)
Appease the appetite with achievement and strive.
(Get off the couch and do something with your life.)
Quench your thirst on accomplished goals.
Happiness will come as balance makes corrections.
Your inner self will grow.
Pay attention to your reflection, the mirror never lies.
Break cycles of predictability.
Welcome solidarity for the sake of everything we
hold sacred; family, new creativity, fresh ideas,
growth and reveal. Expression wants to be accepted,
new voices want to be heard. Hate and distain
remain at the bottom of this plane of existence.
Display qualities that signify a dignified individual.
Portray a being of immaculate perception,
see the errors in your wake.
What is left behind in your steps,
is the Legend you'll make.

...

or
forget all that and just write a bunch
of really cool guitar riffs.

Ball of regret

What's goin' on?
Why are you so upset?
Why do you waste your time?
How did you not see this coming?
Did you think it was just going to pass you by?
Have you even figured out why you're so unhappy?
But more importantly, have you figured out how to
change this feeling of anger and sadness into days of
deep breaths, well rested, calm and collected, where
you're not affected, by mere thoughts of the past or
words that could trigger pain and mental chaos?
Are you done crying? . . . Are you done blaming?
Have you considered, maybe you're a touch insane
to get that wrapped up in something you suspected
all long was never gonna pan out for the better?
Are you done beating yourself up and
dragging yourself through the gutter?
Or would you rather mope instead?
Are you done giving up?
Well?

Adrift in Dream

Carry me away to the light, carry me away in dream,
carry me away to where piano notes take flight, where
I can see this magnificent world free and clear.
No more distress, gone is the mess that encumbers
me. There's a line between life and the billowy cloud
in the sky where I'd like to be, walk with me.

Carry me away in time, adrift in my mind, where I could
get lost for awhile, where I'd dare to smile and it not feel
misplaced or vulnerable to let happiness breathe. Let me
see the ones I love, and the ones I've lost, in the lands
of ripe leaves and majestic, poetic mountain peaks.

Carry me away to a peaceful scenery with a breeze
filled with musical melody, bird song and bee's honey.
I could float at wind speed within angels reach, like riding
the stitched seam of warm rays penetrating brilliant skies,
warming my body as I fly, close enough to graze the tops
of brightly colored summer wheat with my fingertips, like
eagles who once believed they were the kings of God's
creation without a destination, only the freedom to just be-
adrift in dream

Beautiful girl

Hey there beautiful girl, you impress me,
you knock me out
and mean the world to me,
more than I could ever put into words,
but I'd like to try.
With all guards down, straight from the heart;
you shook my world from the first moment I met you.
I remember I couldn't stop kissing you while you
spoke. you just smiled and let me, with your arms
around me, trying to continue the conversation,
as if I wasn't distracting.
I could tell you you're adorable or sexy or beautiful
and pretty, but those words, as monumental as they
are, just can't fully deliver in ways I need them to.
but like I said, I'll try.
your *adorable* for the amazingly cute little girl
inside that loves to cuddle while she stares at
me with those loving vulnerable eyes.
you're *sexy* for all the curves I can't even
speak of without blushing on the inside.
you're *beautiful* for all that you are in heart, your
patience and laughter, your caring, giving spirit, your
body and mind and your children are all what makes you
whole and shine as *beautiful* when you enter a room.
And *pretty*? I kiss your cheek when we make love so I
can see the jaw dropping girl the world sees, as if you
were walking by me, so pretty naturally, making me
wish I knew her, what makes her happy, on the inside,
who makes her smile. Do I even have the guts to ask
her to look directly at me? Who does she put her arms
around when she wants love? And then I come back to
reality and see this pretty girl staring at me, kissing
me, so fucking pretty, I don't know how I got so lucky.
god has truly blessed me. sincerely.

Don't

Don't jump into it too quick.
Don't get married just for the sake of it.
Don't mix finances with love and certainly,
don't expect anything more than a cut-throat
war when you're tryin to get out of it.
Don't give in to anger or it will consume
you and rot your core.
Don't be in a rush to have children, enjoy the
time you two have together, unencumbered by
distractions, feel free to fuck on the kitchen floor.
Don't stay if you see signs of hate, manipulation and lies.
Don't stay if the sex ain't that great or you're often
denied. It'll never get better at a later date.
Don't stay if she doesn't treat you like a king or
she's not affectionate, trust me, you'll regret it.
Don't bring up old fights, old flames or things from
the past, that's a good way to get a foot in your ass.
And above all
Don't forget what brought you two together. Remember
how much you love her, cherish her, hold her and warm
her heart. Always be a gentlemen and let her know she's
world's apart, the angel of light that lifted the dark,
and her smile- gets you through the hardest
parts of your day. This is the only way.

Don't fucking forget.

Toe to Toe

It's never easy getting back on your feet, especially
after you've been knocked the fuck out for an eight
count thirteen rounds deep. It took every friend
I had to help me reason with the landslide of fate
that had buried me. The choice was made, to get my
head on straight, to deal with the immense pain and
honestly, I saw no reason to keep on going. Betrayal
and hurt ran so deep, it was overflowing internally.
I found myself face down in my hands trying to
swallow all that I had counted on, coming to an
end. I went into shock, denial, disbelief and all
the while going off the deep end. Confusion and
madness, anger and sadness, even moments in the
middle of the night I'd wake in utter frustration.
With the uncertainty of tomorrow, overwhelming sadness
and gut-wrenching sorrow, controlling every breath I
borrowed, there was no chance for me to pull out a win.
I would only go down again, so I threw the towel in.
Just then, I slowly came to, focused on a master plan
to land on my feet again. To stand and demand more
from myself, command my emotions to take back seat,
give me a fighting chance to figure out my dreams, to
see if the seams that came unstitched were repairable.
It was apparent and undeniable, I was on the floor
begging for the bell to save me, but God gave me one
last breath. I stood up to take another swing and sure
enough I had it in me, a life defining moment of clarity.
Fire ran through me. I could see a victory through
the haze of scumbaggery. Fuck the excuses. No more
ruses. No more tears for bruises. Take a punch like
a real man. Get the fuck back up and live again.

System Overload

Hope cannot rescue the tortured mind. 'Wish & will'
cannot correct the damaged drive. Only time can
repair a system overload. For inside, there are sensitive
mechanisms that make up the 'Heart and Mind'
and within the system lies a delicate balance of
'Pain and Overcome'. Sometimes you can re-route a
solution, other times, the wiring is so fried and so ladened
with hurt, tragedy and betrayal, the load locks down
the mainframe, short circuiting the brain, knocking
out all the lights, blanketing the unprotected mind
from feeling anything, including normalcy ever again.
That's where 'Fear and Heartbreak' have made it past
the firewall and manifest in the corner, as a poison
in the forward compartment, uncontested where no
one can stop it, and if never corrected, the virus will
create a systematic breakdown and spread throughout
the body, infecting, overloading the hosts capacity,
manufacturing 'Loathe and Jealousy' blowing delicate
circuitry that'll sicken the entire individual, even the
family, sometimes spreading into society. Prevention
is key, but no one plans to get their heart broken, so
'Pain' is to be handled yet again, systematically.
1. Re-check your connection; with friends and goals.
2. Breathe deep; join a gym and get some sleep.
3. Surround yourself with ones that nurture
and believe, and in time you'll see, 'Overcome'
will be back on line, eventually.

Mommy's little Angel

She softly kisses her newborn's tiny ear. The light sweetened scent of baby skin gently wisps into her nose, triggering her protective, nurturing instincts and warming her young mothering heart, deep within.

The first-time mother, closes her eyes with her lips pressed ever so gently against her child's head and whispers;

"You've saved my life little one, in fact, you've changed it forever. I'm so glad you're here. I love you more than you could possibly know, thank you."

(*15 years later*)

"Are you fucking kidding me!?
Are you trying to kill me!?
Get the FUCK in the car.... NOW!!
And give me your phone, you spoiled ungrateful bitch. I AM GOING TO BEAT YOUR GODDAM ASS WHEN WE GET HOME!! You are gonna be the death of me someday. Thank you for the stress you have caused me. sincerely. Thank you.

Last Chance

Picture your last fucking breath. You're dying, looking
at death in the next few minutes. This is how it's going
to end, this is how it's happening, nothing like you
thought it would be. Nothing like you imagined.
Blood coming out your nose. Piss, shit and vomit all over
your toes. There's no getting out of it. You've begged God
a million times before to save you from yourself and give
you more time to journey, achieve and explore, but you
ignored the signs and gifts extended and kept on living the
way you wanted and not the way he intended. Now, you're
worried, cuz there are children involved who will surely
suffer, who will be ever so sad as your death will even
shock your lover. It'll complicate their ride and slow them
down as they drown in mourn, but you were fore warned.
They'll fall to their knees and lose their dreams of family
events with Dad. They'll watch that future fade away in
seconds as you're lowered into your grave. But at least you
did it your way. right? You stubborn stupid fuck, not quite.
You fought so hard to not be a slave, but that's exactly how
you were played. A slave to your habits. Owned by your
desires. You died by your own fucking hand, alone, at
night. Temptations were planted and you took everything
for granted. Imagine if you had just listened to the voices
inside, trying to save you from eternal heartbreak, but now
it's too late for a song and a dance, here come the crows.
that was your last chance.

Us

Just as manifest destiny led the 19th century,
inevitably, more so, incredibly, the masses, it has been
discovered, can be led to a victory. Let's insist we gather
our senses and do what's best for Us. Stop pretending
the few that screw and lie represent all of Us.
It's our own fault if we don't change Us.
Let's at least tell our children we tried,
that we didn't go down without a fight.
So proudly we've fallen. Like Rick Astley said,
'destiny's callin'.
We've become monetary cattle, born an bred,
accepting distraction on a worldwide scale.
Words are twisted and minced like vomited kisses
forced to be swallowed like holiday beverages.
But it's the leverage they use to own you and abuse their
power any way they choose. Guess what? You lose!
Don't pretend you care for me or my family, I've
watched you spit on our own blood and aid our
enemy. Conspiracy? Don't even come near me.
Ask not what I can do for you,
stop splitting this world in two..
we all bleed the same blood,
I'm tired of the same rut.
Let's cut the shit and change Us.

Message in a Bottle

This is a message in a bottle, a time capsule,
a letter for tomorrow, a reminder after I've left here,
that I've always held dearly the ones around me,
close to my heart, blood or not.
You were the magic that gave me purpose and
brought warmth and clarity into my life. Your
soul's light helped guide me to be the man I
wanted to be through darkened times.
Your laughter is my treasure and echoes in my memories.
Everything you were, kept a smile on my face and
rescued me from misery's deep. Your faces etched in
my mind, led the way through cloudy days when the
sun didn't shine so bright on my side of the street.
I had many goals in my life and one of them was
to a be surrounded by ones that loved me.
It was a gift like no other and my pleasure-
to be your uncle, your friend, your brother
and your father.

Father Time

Please, I'm asking you to slow down just a touch.
You're going too fast, and just when things start going well,
you're suddenly in a rush. I'm not asking to savor the flavor
or cater to dreams so out of reach its insane to fathom. I'm
just saying I can't get things done any faster, while you're
blasting past me like a dragster. I'm chasing dreams as I
age, I'm planting seeds late, I already know what you're
gonna say, "nothing ever seems to go my way". Exactly, and
all the more reason to slow the fuck down and let me try
again. I'm not asking for much. Maybe a day where there's
a family, finally standing, together sharing, a dinner
or lunch, with my children and my beautiful woman
laughing at a picnic, staring at me, spitting watermelon
seeds, drinking iced tea and making memories, but
you're going to fast for me to make this dream a reality.
This shit takes time. Please, I beg of you, don't let me
die without getting to see my children one last time.

The Adventures of Dickstain & Captain Fuckstick

We find our heroes wandering through a
foreign land, searching for sustenance so grand,
it was said to be out of fucking hand.
"Don't touch anything Dickstain." said the older brother.
"Don't worry I won't Fuckstick! I'm just looking for
something. Something I know is here or was in tale. It
was said to be red and green with mighty purple hairs."
He said as they tip-toed with extreme care, for they were
in the lair of the pig nosed, cow-bellied momma bear.
"Wow. Red and green. I bet that's quite a mean...
Shhh! I hear someone coming. Quick Dickmeat, hide."
"Don't call me that, I'm not a queer."
"Whatever Dickstain. I have no doubt
you take it in the rear."
"Oh, good one Captain Fuckstick, did you stay up all
night thinking that one up? Now shut the fuck up and
look for a shiny tin. It holds the treasure we seek. The
treasure of pleasure that reeks beyond measure. An aroma
so alluring it's captives fall under it's spell. I'm talking
about the fabled deer frozen in headlights look. A tight
as fuck alien abduction of epic proportion. The reason
Pink Floyd is on the moon and Led is in the Zepplin."
"Hark! I found the tin. It's under Momma bear's
fatass chin, along with some percocets."
"Be sure not to wake the bitch, she'll rip off our nuts
and throw us in a ditch. Quick, take what we need and
leave the rest under her saggy-ass, dilapidated breasts.
I can't stand the shriek of shock of us in her nest. Last
time she caught me, she made me her cleaning bitch,
fuck that shit. Hey... Fuckstick, do we even have fire?"

"Don't worry about me Dickstain, I brought a pipe
and a light. I wish you'd give me some fuckin'
credit. Tonight we go out in a blaze of glory.
We'll be higher than fuck 'til morning.
Now let's get out of here before we get caught.
End of fucking story."

Rainwater

Wait to see how much we've collected.
Is it clean or is it tainted all the way through?
Once its gone we'll need more, we always do.
When the well runs dry we'll have to dig deeper to get
our hands wet again. We'll surely die without it.
It's a necessity of life. Even children understand
the value and importance of it.
There are times I've bathed in it and other
times I've witnessed droughts.
There are times I've prayed for it and
thanked God for the amounts.
From which deposit will we be taking it from?
Most of us just expect it to come.
This poem has been about money,
don't tell me you're that fucking dumb.

Woman

It'll vary from who you're speaking with, but don't let
it fool you. Don't let what you hear, even the words
right out of a woman's mouth, steer you. They are real
easy to read, and they test you, to trigger the best in
you and are more than happy to misguide you. It's in
their nature to find a suitor who can best deliver and
meet the level of their individual rescue. Just as a man
is easy to please while vocalizing more of his needs
by grunting his way to satisfaction, a woman needs
communication as they work more from intellect and
compassion than breaking things in moronic frustration.
They may sit quiet in design and look sweet on the outside,
but they are carnivores for sure with a hellacious appetite.
Their list of needs is long and depends on the girl and
where shes from. They all want a great nest to prepare
for their offspring, however some demand a diamond
ring and the musical notes of fancy belongings.
There are some who are just grateful for your love
and companionship, but the one thing they all have
in common is no matter what's dictated from society
or the woman's individuality; they all want a man to
be a fucking man, take her by the hand and demand
her love in the moonlight. She wants you to find
the toughest way to be tender, the roughest way to
handle her while caressing the affection out of her.
Grunt, but don't fart, there's a difference, she
wants a man not a frat house shitbrick.
Help her, but stay out of her way. Do the dishes but
make sure you follow through and put them away. If
you do anything for her, don't do it half-assed or she'll
always remember you as the lame douche who couldn't
handle being a real man and rock that sweet ass.

Fast Lane

Bright lights, hookers card, title deed, freeze-frame,
high stakes, play hard, fast game, high heels, fast lane,
lip sync, poker face, lipstick, rich bitch, money grip,
cheat scheme, bleach blonde, big spender, bartender,
next round, wallet drain, crown royal, whiskey dick,
ass flip, sucka made, every day, cocaine, new chips,
big hit, new room, credit line, headline, man wins big,
woman leaves on a cruise line.
Now broke, bank choke, seized card, alley bound,
ripped shirt, dirty flirt, drunk and hurt, call dad,
couldn't hurt. Cash sent, with a note, come home before
you're found, tied up, in a trunk, curled up, in a box,
with a fuckin bullet hole, face down in a toilet bowl.
how ya gonna get home?
maybe I should just fly back,
or
buy a gun to get back, all the money from the set back.
smoke crack, man up and fight back. talk shit,
slap bitch, walk rich, act like you own it.
walkin' tall through the front door pumpin,
loaded gun on the front hip, heart's thumpin,
out of my skin, bout to come gunnin'.
mack a bitch, from behind and blow it.
what was I thinkin, cops gonna clink me
better buy a ticket for a bus ride,
throw the gun past the tree line,
must be outta my, fuckin' mind.
I ain't tellin' not a single friend.
fuckin' money changes. It's true what they say,
let that shit stay in Vegas.

Forever Broken

Where do we draw the line? It's okay some of the time?
Deliver us from evil, but don't give us directions.
Save me from myself, but mind your own fucking business.
Entertain us, but don't be offensive.
Tell us the truth, but not if it hurts.
Knowledge is exclusive, you must be entitled.
Seats are limited, there's absolutely no vacancy.
Oh wait, you have money? Right this way.
You're to blame, you should be ashamed. You
need to repent, you need to be saved.
Creation didn't make you, you're a mistake.
Dream big, imagine grand.
It's unacceptable how you think.

Afflicted with sadness, we drink from the chalice
of madness to cure us, only to become poisoned
again. The cycle completes and repeats itself til were
a society built to only reproduce broken beings.

Just like You

Some say I was born defeated. Others say I'm different; that there's pieces to the puzzle that are just plain missing. But they're going off a scale, going off some kinda chart, as if an individual's magnificence and magnitude could be magically measured in colors and bars. I'm eleven years old. I know what I like, I know what I love, I can remember things no one else does. In fact, I'm gifted in ways that only my mother can see, but that's only because you've never spent any time with me. I'm not the same as others they'd have you believe, because the lights are too bright or it's too loud to hear my self think, but honestly, these sound like words I've heard from everybody else. So what, I don't like my steak to touch my peas. That doesn't mean there's anything wrong with me. I'm special to you, I'm normal to me. No reason to talk to me condescendingly. I need love, I feel pain, I think the world of my family just as anyone else would. I want to climb the highest mountains and fly to the dark side of the moon just like you. I sit on the couch and eat ice cream and have a laugh or two then scratch my pet when I'm thru. I cry when you're mean to me, I'm sad when you don't care, because all I wanna do is love you and show you I'm important too. I'm pretty sure that's the way you'd want it to be for you. I'm different in some ways, I'll agree, but I'm just like you in more ways than you can see.

Labels

So let me get this right, sadness is blue and
seeing red is anger, and frustration could
be maroon. just saying, stay with me.
You can also be green with envy, or white from fright.
Yellow is the color of a coward and the sickly.
Black is empty, dark and evil,
Grey is dismal and depressed.
And brown always stood for the ground we
walk on and reminds us all of a pile of shit.
So where is all the happiness? I'd hate to give my
kid a box of these shitty, depressing ass crayons.

Last I checked, red also meant warmth, sexy, and hot.
Blue can also mean cold, but not if the skies are
clear and the sun is shining bright, then blue
is the only hue the sky has ever known.
Yellow is the sun that gives everything life,
the daffodil, the sunflower, the exotic orchid's
stamen, that's the very important part inside.
Rainbows are majestic, brown is rustic, and black has
always been the sickest color for the coolest car coming
down the road. White is billowy and pillowy and who
can forget the beauty of snow and its wintery scenery.
But more importantly, it seems there's more
to a color then what it's been deemed.
There's diversity and depth, more than what's been said.
Seems to me, you can never judge a color by the label
in which its kept.

Breathe

Living, comes at a price. Problems are always quick to arise. They ripen with cost and compromise our thoughts and push our patience to the brink of our sanity. Although we try to remain stress-free, it's their incessant ability to inevitably thrive and be seen as obstacles of impossibility- unfortunately, weighing heavily on the mind. This should come as no surprise. Even the best of us who try diligently to avoid the hassles of life can still get hit from behind with this overwhelming bullshit in disguise, such as 'a like' on social media from a woman who ain't your wife.

As we all know, problems are trouble in waiting. They gather momentum and with no limits or boundaries they come at the absolute worst possible time, like a big snowball of shit rolling downhill just waiting to fuck up your life. In an instant you can be swept up in a tornado of anger, stress and hopelessness, (and now I'm being serious, stop waiting for a punchline) with no answer in sight. and you can bet your last fucking dollar, this shit will hit the fan just as you're ready to call it a night. Ah, but here's the magnificence in nature's genius- the free gift of a new day is upon us; a new sunrise can cleanse us. What once seemed hopeless now suddenly has answers. What was utterly frustrating, now has rescue and resolve. So I can't stress this enough.

"Take a fuckin breath. Re-fuckin-lax yourself. Wait til morning for a new day to come; some way, some how the universe seems to open a door and shine a light, on the unanswerable problems we couldn't see the answer to, at night.

...and quickly get off social media.

__Damage Plan__

To future generations; we're handing down problems
that never got fixed. Greed got the best of us. It's not
that complex. Everything has been about profit, less
overhead and now instead of a world teaming with life,
the world is in shambles as we scramble to survive.
We know we fucked up and we're all to blame. We put
politicians in charge and let them play their sinful,
corrupt, scumbag games. They thank the schemers
who fund their vacations, then turn their heads to
the poison being made. It's in our food, our air and
in our waters. It's in the lands that feed our cattle.
There's not a child or animal on the planet that
doesn't have Teflon in it's blood. The fact is you're the
children suffering from the damage we've done.

So here's the damage plan.

Revamp the entire wiring for the aspiring to admire
the lands they stand on. Demand more from the
Commander to enact a plan for a cleaner future
instead of the random handshake that'll talk shit
and mansplain how they took your nest-egg, or deny
how the planet is dying and crying out. Were over-
fishing, over-mining, over-eating and stripping her
down to her core. Trust me, she can't take anymore.
Heal wounds with your enemies, it'll all work
better when you're friendly. Then pray to god.
and when you're done, pray some more.
You're gonna need it.

<u>Sleep</u>

Sleep?
I'll get all the sleep I need when I die.
You get 60 years and then some to climb
the highest mountains you can find.
Sleep?
Sleep is for babies to grow
and for drug addicts who don't know how to find their
way home. Look around you, friends and family are
gone. Time is lost and flying bye so fast. I remember
holding my daughter as she took her first breath. Now
she's in college taking her first test. And I'll be in a
box before ya know it. If I blow it and let up on the
gas for even a second, I'll miss my chances to connect
and correct the life I've wasted, to make me who
I want to be, shape my destiny,
leave a legacy for my name and family.

I'm not done being me. I got 6 outta 8 cylinders firing right
now. There's not a mountain I can't climb or a sky that's
high enough for the rocket that's about to take the fuck off.
Sleep is for dreaming, life is what's happening. I'm 48, I've
wasted enough time believing in lucky charms and wishing
wells, fortune-tellers and magic spells. I'm done waiting.
No more dreaming. Fuck sleeping.

Demonfeed

Is your soul worth saving?
The Demon that lives inside your heart and mind says
otherwise. It scratches at the back of your eyes, where
bad decisions, arrogance and dark memories lie. Then
seeds of failure are planted, slowly growing, poisoning
the mind, making you question if you're good enough
deep inside. You become disconnected. In the mirror
you'll seem fine, but in time your inner self will cry
out in pain, in shame, for the crimes you've committed
against yourself and others, and you'll realize-
you are the only one to blame.
Denial is a child's game.
And now the demon's at play,
slowly tearing away at the fiber that made you once
believe in yourself, haunting you, reminding you of
what you could have done
and what you should never have done.
It slowly murders you for fun.
It'll talk you into believing you're someone, you're not.
As if you're evil and twisted,
even worse, worthless, second guessing,
dissecting the truth, letting him feed on you.
An apocalyptic end will surely come at the hands
of the redemption you'll seek, as you're broken
down to pieces, devoured and weakened, so far
out of repair, you're now in the demon's lair.
He wants the strongest part of your being, the part
that's worth saving, the part that can be sold, now
wallowing in madness and under control by the
voices that pester and pull. You're unsure as self
loathe festers inside and your entire makeup will be
shaken, not partly, but in whole and transformed,
til you'd rather die then live with your own soul.

Caterpillar

A wet chill sat heavily in the morning fog of
the northern forest. Throughout the day, light
rains had gently sprayed their cold mist down
from the clouded gray skies passing by.
It was just another fall morning for the flora and fauna
to wake and find sustenance, although none were
stirring, food was still in abundance. The only sounds
to be heard were the tiny pats of water droplets falling
from branch to branch, finally landing onto loose leaves
that lie on the marshy forest floor. It was a crisp kind
of cold that told all- to stay under leaf, under warmth
of brush, or in the cavernous indentations under the
mountainous formation, away from winds that gust.
and so the morning went on.
Suddenly, I heard a strange, high pitch roar. I quickly
sat up in my tent. The sound seemed to be completely
alien to this part of the land. Faint, but it was growing
near, almost sounded like machinery, in gear.
"No fuckin way" I said out loud as I rushed out of my
tent. And there it was, in plain site, there to ruin in
seconds what took nature lifetimes; a giant black and
yellow Caterpillar. Not the pretty kind that morphs
into butterflies, but the 100 ton kind that ruins lives.
There was nothing I could do. It's sad to watch these
majestic trees fall, but they should've known, how dare
they grow so tall, this is a perfect site for a much needed,
humanity saving, new and improved shopping mall.

No Fuckin Way

No fuckin way did she just say what I think she said.
No fuckin way is my day going to shit after all that I did.
No fucking way is this happening to me; of all the things,
of all the days, of all the ways, the universe just loves
fucking me. I literally should just walk hunched over,
so at a moments notice I can quickly bend over and
let the world just pound away at my ass. Just Fuck me
over and over because this is my life. Not just today, I
was dry fucked yesterday and the day before that. My
momma dropped me on my head at the age of three.
That bitch chose to save the groceries instead of me.
Now you believe me?
I'm afraid to read my emails, or answer my phone cuz
it's going to be some motherfucker with a 19 inch dong
waiting to shove it where that shit don't belong.
Car accident? lane closed? pants ripped? drop your
key in a sewer? Of course. Identity theft? no problem.
Divorced for the second time? Screwed on your
taxes? Late for work? Sure, why not? I got this.
In fact, let's get pulled over and get the cop to join in
the fucking chorus.
"There's no fucking way this is happening to me today."

Embedded

If you've ever hit rock bottom and it's a sad habit for
some, whether divorced, bad choices, or drugs; poverty,
lost job or some other fuckin reason you're on the
bottom rung, then unfortunately you know how the air
tastes down there. The forgotten feeling. The shallow
breathing. The sleepless nights, bad diets and miserable
fights. The run riot in your mind every fuckin night
how you tried and failed and just wish you could die
from the embarrassment on such a huge scale...
Slow. No blood flow to the heart. No get up and go. ur
whole world has fallin apart and then some. It's been
all takin with no reciprocation or consideration. Your
Inspiration is gone, your eyes half open from obliteration,
afraid to see what else could possibly go wrong...
and then it happens. A doorway of hope opens. You
hesitate, for sure, but for some reason it's pure. it
takes you in, and fills your heart back up from the
spill that tore you apart and pumps more than blood
back into you. Restores your faith and sanity unlike
the gravity that pulled you down. It's a rescue, and
just like that you're better than before, fully restored.
given new life, a new fight, with a sincerity and love
from none other than a woman and her son.
I can't thank you enough for all the love.
You're in my heart forever. Embedded.

Contact

I've come here from a distant place, to tell you all
something unthinkable. Why I have to is actually
incredible, almost ridiculously unimaginable. Allow
me to explain. I've traveled through space and time
to ask you a couple very important questions.
In all you're work and search for what's out there in the
great beyond, deep in outer space, deep past the stars;
with all the time you spend and the focus you lend on
imagining an exotic, exciting world with different types
of beings, new places to see, with creatures tied into the
symbiotic structure of it's existence; like trees that need
the wind and animals that need the trees, where the
inhabitants of such a magical planet live off their land and
survive off their wonderfully enriched seas, where cities
are majestic, so much so, their beauty is awe inspiring,
what is it your looking for? Is it cool alien technology,
like everything you need at your fingertips with just a
touch on a sort of thin, computerized pad thing? With
all the time you spend gazing into the stars wondering
what's afar, sadly, and I say this with a heavy heart, you've
wasted your precious time. You've completely ignored
all the glory of your own life, in your own world with all
the different, magnificent, species and races around you.
This is a warning, this is a sign, before it's gone, go to
the ones who cherish your love and your precious time.
And for what it's worth, all the amazing things you seek
are right in front of your eyes, right here on Earth.

A Masterpiece of Disaster

You're a masterpiece of disaster, you're misery is divine.
You're elegance in brutality is magnificent in design.
A cannibalistic overlord who eats their prey alive.
A dainty, goddess of desire, a hellish angel in disguise.
Don't kid yourself, you're a real fuckin bitch inside.
A manufacturer of real pain, a relentless sadistic drain,
a sentinel of exsanguination with repetitious sustain.
Next victim, next sin, next crown, next kin.
You're reliably unreliable and incredibly unscrupulous.
A materialistic, unrealistic, thick as fuck, dumb
as a brick temptress, living to impress and feed
her massive ego. A threat to any throne.
You're the hellish pyre that burns the brightest.
Instinctual as a killing virus. Your innocence was
buried under earth and stone the day you uttered,
"I deserve more than anyone".
You're reputation is undeniable. Your conniving smiles
are insidiously fake to the bone. You're notoriously
ungrateful. A user and everyone knows. The queen of lies
with an insatiable appetite, who's adoration has expired.
No one likes you, they just want to fuck you.
You're predictable and transparent. Lower than
the snake that slithers through brush.
You are without a doubt, the epitome of 'Cunt'.
Your actions are smoke and mirrors. You're phony with
a fake as fuck laugh. You sound insane, and are a flat out
drunken bore. Your love of money and greed to please
your financial need, is literally the definition of whore.

Everyone's a Critic II

It amazes me, even astounds me. I'm blown away by
the audacity, the pretentious capacity, the belittling
and self-crowned, self-inflated, wanna-be, upper
echelon, peanut gallery. So much to say, so much
input, so much greater knowledge of the world,
existence and it's beings. Thank God your critique
is around to lead us, to let us all know where we, the
lower crust, the shit dust stand; below the elitist.
It's funny, and not just in a
"Writer trying to make himself feel better by writing a
poem in a smart ass way about people who put down
his writings" kinda way, no, it's funny how I've stood
face to face with those who have looked down their nose
and have had so much to say, and without trying, I've
noticed the anomalies, deformities, and the ugly- the
crusted crooked teeth, bad breath, wrinkled, out of
shape, aging mouth these critiques have come out of.
There's no two-ways about it. Seriously, these aren't
burns. This I surmise, you haven't done anything in
your life and, I'm embarrassed to say this; but it's been
a downhill ride every since you left high school. Perhaps
this has been a serendipitous encounter, one that'll
help me better my repartee, or maybe, I'll continue to
write the droll you so despise and not give a fuck about
your views of my candor. So let's not do this anymore,
there's the door, please leave. Sadly, you're exhaustingly
unimportant to me, a petulant fucking 'nobody'.

Explosive Diarrhea

Just when you thought you've heard it all,
some shit crosses your path that doesn't just shock
you- it rocks the very foundation of sanity, blowing
your mind with a level of unbelievable that surpasses
absurdity by miles, landing in the vicinity of stupidity
but closer to "Are you fucking kidding me!?"
You think, what could be the reason.
So you bring it up for conversation and it becomes an
argument on line that's explosive as diarrhea with C-4,
like a tampon in the back door yanked out just before
the taco six-pack hits the floor, like a shot outta
Moby Dick's asshole. BAM! There she blows!
Instant shit show.
Anger and hate spew, no versions of answers can
be used, just know-it-all keyboard warrior judges
with racial prejudice and a penchant for speaking
as an authority. Suddenly you drop the angle you
stand for, you speak up and declare war on the
fact that there's no common sense anymore.
It seemed like the most legitimate, decent, correct,
reason for speaking up, but its regurgitated
through dialogue like ass vomit throw-up. That's
the last time I ask for an opinion on facebook.

Printed in the United States
By Bookmasters